Abilities for Those with Disabilities

Teaching Adults Life Skills

On a Computer

S.J. Marier

STEP BY STEP INSTRUCTIONS

TO TEACH ADULTS COMPUTERS AND LIFE SKILLS

I would like to thank:

Windsor Volunteers for Literacy

For graciously funding the initial project that lead to the publication of this book. Their funding provides seed money for various literacy projects in our community.

September 2011

TABLE OF CONTENTS

INTRODUCTION..7

Abilities for Those with Disabilities..................................8

Teaching Adults Life Skills 8

Why is this Material Needed ? 12

Teaching Life Skills And Literacy With The Aid Of A Computer 13

Finding Computers 16

Funding 17

Who Can Volunteer? 17

Special Needs for Computers 19

Programs Available for Learners.............................20

Student's Original Works 22

Suggested Topics for Small Classes 26

Preparing Assignments for a Classroom Setting.............29

Clear Writing..30

Goal Setting for Students..34

ASSIGNMENTS 36

Class Assignments 37

GRAMMAR 39

Punctuation...40

Ways to Figure out Words 41

Making Changes 43

Verb Selection 45

Add Endings to These Root Words 46

How To Write Personal Stories 47

Canadians Overweight 48

Chief Tecumseh 49

COMPUTER SKILLS 50

Computer Class - Progress: 51

Tab Keys 53

Internet 54

Saving Money 56

Using the Internet- Basic Skills 59

E-mail 60

The Internet 61

Email for those who use Yahoo 63

Blogging 65

Devices we Use Today 67

Cell Phones 68

Working with Photographs on Your Computer 69

LIFE SKILLS 71

Fire Safety In The Kitchen 72

Safe Medication Use..74

Reading a Newspaper 75

Fuel up for Spring Sports 76

Living With Diabetes 77

The Beginning of Summer 78

Sunscreen 79

Tips for Winter Safety 80

Identity Theft - Protect Yourself...81

Phony Charities 82

Shopping at the Grocery Store 83

Power Outage...85

Food Safety Basics..87

Sanitation...88

Flu 90

Add Regular physical Activity To Your Daily Routine 91

Shopping and Cooking Healthy Meals 92

Comparative Shopping and Use of Tables.........................94

ASSESSMENT..95

Assessment for New Learners...96

Numbers and Letters...99

NUMBERS AND LETTERS 100

Numbers Exercise 101

Using Letters 103

Holiday Gift Giving 104

New Years 105

Things I did over the Christmas Season: 106

Halloween in North America 107

Opposites 108

Fill in the Blanks 109

RECIPES AND OTHER ACTIVITIES 111

Mr. Bean is Funny 111

Beef Noodle Chop Suey 112

Wrap It The Way You Like 113

What did put in your Wrap? 114

Picnic 115

INTRODUCTION

Abilities for Those with Disabilities

<u>Teaching Adults Life Skills</u>

Literacy has played a very important part in my life. I would like to celebrate my love for literacy. We all have dreams of becoming an integrated part of our modern society. Why not, nobody needs to be left out in the cold. Everyone can be taught with a little encouragement and support.

Nobody needs to say,

"I am too old to learn! Nobody will take the time to teach me computers, cell phones, important life skills or any of those new gadgets in my life!"

Here is an opportunity. Take the challenge to learn. Take the time to teach others. I am revealing all the secrets I have learned over the past 25 years. There are those who need that little extra something. They need support and encouragement. Maybe you know someone special that needs that extra push. Given the chance, anyone can learn and become part of our rapidly changing technological world.

Our students know the difference between a Windows 98 and a Windows 7 computer. They know which cell phone makes calls, which gets them connected to the internet and which one takes pictures. Each of them have downloaded pictures off a digital camera. We have discussed many technological advancement that affect our lives in our class. We teach basic life skills that make a difference between a dinner or a burnt egg. Don't settle for something mediocre. Take the challenge to learn what we have learned through reading this book. You will be amazed.

Each of our exercises can be printed and used by anyone. There are no copywriters on these products. This enables anyone interested in these exercises to use them for whatever purpose they choose. These exercises were developed in Windsor, Ontario. The Volunteers of The Downtown Centre, Community Living Windsor welcome your interest in this Program. Working with individuals who want to improve their literacy skills is very rewarding.

In 1969 I started volunteering with Literacy as a teenager. I worked with inner city children that didn't have a chance unless someone brought their reading skills up to speed. I drove to Chene Street in Detroit, every Saturday morning to help those kids learn to read and write. It paid off; they would have been left out. Those third graders were able to catch up to the rest of their class. They taught me a thing or two about life.

One little girl took care of her four younger siblings every single day after school and put them to bed at night while mom worked. She taught me that being street smart was essential for her survival. We both learned in 1969, that we were grateful that the riots were over in Detroit. We had important business to take care of. She needed to stay in school to get ahead in life. I needed to finish High School and go on to College.

I still have my very first Certificate of Recognition:

Issued by the Detroit Metropolitan School District

Signed by the Chairman of the School Board back in 1969

13 inner city children signed the back of the Certificate.

My favorite student left her phone number. I wish Frances the best. That little girl just needed a little time to herself away from those brothers and sisters to learn.

In 1987 I started volunteering and working for the Windsor Public Library Adult Literacy Program. As a <u>Laubach Tutor</u>, I worked one on one, teaching those individuals with low literacy skills how to read. It was very rewarding work. I held various duties within the organization including publishing a newsletter, publicizing the program to the community and being instrumental in recruiting developmentally handicapped adults into computer programs. I worked with three individuals during the course of 10 years using the Laubach each-one-teach- one method. I felt I could do more. I wanted to make a difference in the lives of many adults that lacked literacy skills.

In 1999 our computer class began. We started out with old computers, Windows 95 computers. There were even older computers, those that just had DOS on them. Computers were connected to screens and key boards that did not belong to each other. It did not matter, as long as the computer turned on and off. As long as the students could type, the program continued. I enjoy working with the computers, fixing them, reconnecting the wires, making sure the keyboard works with the hard drive it was connected with. I must have spent half the class time fixing those old computers. Those were the only computers we had.

Anybody else would have discarded them as junk. They worked; we pieced odds and ends of various computers together. The result of all this effort was running a computer class at the Downtown Centre, Community Living Windsor. People flocked to our class; we kept busy making assignments for Monday. Since those early days, we have received generous donations to upgrade our computers. We are very grateful to our benefactors.

Three years ago, The Downtown Centre moved. We now have a spacious and private computer lab. The door is shut every Monday at 1 pm. Everyone who comes to the drop- in center knows, the computer class is in session. We do not want to be disturbed.

Today, we are proud to have three new, state of the art, <u>Windows 7</u> Computers. We still are lacking in the most critical component of this program, we need more volunteers. We have other students who need a lot of attention. They cannot type yet nor have no idea how to use a mouse. Most of our students learn very quickly. They need a volunteer to help them initially on a one on one basis. We do not promote this as a one on one program. It is difficult to turn someone away that wants to learn.

Why is this Material Needed ?

There is a lack of available material for low level learners, adults with little computer literacy skills and those with special needs. The software that is available is very costly or difficult for the learner to comprehend. Working with computers with people who have developmental disabilities can be challenging but at the same time very rewarding . The material and suggestions have been used with successful results with special needs learners that have had little or no experience with computers.

You will also see lessons used in classroom situations for learners who have progressed at a remarkable rate. There are examples of types of work that can used for first time computer users. A variety of learners can benefit from this program. It is a matter of choosing which type of learning environment you wish to cater to. It might be a classroom situation, one – on –one tutoring, or over seeing adults typing a bit.

Individuals or groups of adults who could benefit from this program include:

- Adults who are intellectually challenged
- People living in group homes
- Individuals with low literacy skills
- Seniors who have had little or no computer experience
- People with hearing impairments
- English as a Second Language learners

Teaching Life Skills And Literacy With The Aid Of A Computer

Not all of us have the potential to get a college degree. Some individuals have very basic or no apparent literacy skills. This should not deter them from using a computer keyboard and mouse. After six years of working with adults in a group setting or individual situations, we would like to share our experiences so that other volunteers or literacy coordinators can benefit. Adult learners with little or no literacy skills can be part of the computer era. We will show many successful methods which will peak a person's desire to excel in their computer skills.

It's important to find the base line of a person's skills. This is especially true when working with adults that have not been challenged for a long time.

- What skills are they are able to perform?
- What activity holds their interest?
- What are their goals?

It is important to build up their confidence to improve on these skills. The ultimate goal is to give positive reinforcement that they are learning something new and important.

At some point it is possible to introduce new skills if the person has a means of assimilating these skills with something they already know. The task they are learning may seem small, recognizing letters, counting coins, or telling time. The time it takes to master a skill is not important. They have been told what they were not capable of learning for years. A teaching method, which works for one individual, may not work for another.

One method that works for everyone is positive reinforcement. Learners are thrilled with taking home some example of their work They may not show this work to anyone else but there is pride in the fact that they have accomplished some new skill.

Some of the computer programs are basic typing programs that challenge a person's typing skills. A letter may appear or fly across the screen and the student needs to find it on the keyboard. Finding the correct letters is a challenge to learners. At the end of the session, the learner's speed is recorded. The speed is not compared to anybody else's speed but the learner challenges himself to beat their own score.

There are learners who have never touched a keyboard before and are now typing sentences and paragraphs about topics that interest them. Each learner has an area where they need to be challenged. It could be learning money skills, telling time, shopping, reading, basic math or any number of goals they may have to become more independent.

Many learners have goals to become more independent. The critical issue is to capture what they want to learn and with positive reinforcement. Many of them can learn concepts they never thought possible. The key to this is consistent reinforcement in all settings. There are volunteers out there that can be utilized if they were directed to what their specific responsibilities are. Cooking and typing recipes is an example of a life skill that many adults find challenging.

As a volunteer, I have taught a cooking class for 6 years with very basic, ordinary ingredients. All of the learners have immensely enjoyed preparing main dishes, desserts, salads, and many other appetizing recipes. After the preparation, everyone is eager to prepare our menu item of the month at home. The only way they can take this recipe home, is by typing out their own copy. It is a great incentive to get each person typing.

Often in a recipe new computer skills are introduced such as bullets or numbering. We make a point of not introducing too many new computer skills at one time. An example of this may be local concerts, fairs, freedom day festivities. You can have an assignment typed up in advance about local activities coming up, have your learners make a calendar and mark upcoming events, or have them write about their favorite event. Each of these activities introduces a new computer and typing skill.

During the holiday season, everyone loves making cards on the computer. Depending on what type of computer you have in your facility, a card may be made in MS Word using clip art and two columns on a page. There are many programs available for making greeting cards. If someone who is learning to use a mouse may be challenged by finding a clip art and placing it in the card. Some people may type a short greeting for a card. Whatever the occasion is such as a birthday, wedding , Christmas or Valentine's Day, just to mention a few occasions, many are thrilled by making their own card when they are on a budget.

Finding Computers

To get started in a computer program it is not necessary to have the newest computer. Often the older computers that have Windows 95 or 98 are easier to use for a new learner. You may have an interest in finding some computers to start up a program in your organization but your funds are limited.

You will be surprised how many places are upgrading their systems and have no use for their older computers that still work.

Here is a suggestion of places to contact to get used computers donated to you organization.

- Large industrial companies in your area
- Businesses
- Local School boards
- Local Libraries
- Municipal Offices
- Community Support Organizations
- Local Hospitals
- Community Centers

These places may not have any old computers but perhaps they might guide you in another direction.

Funding

Perhaps there are grants available to start up a program in your community. Perhaps money that is available for learners can be used to set up classrooms. Once certainty, if an individual learns how to eat healthy now, exercise properly, shop for the right foods the end costs will be lower as the medical needs of this aging population.

Who Can Volunteer?

What qualifications does a volunteer instructor need to instruct a classroom of special needs learners? The key ingredient is to be caring and patient. A volunteer does not need to be a computer software expert. It is important to know a basic word processing program like MS Word or Word Perfect.

Sometimes you need to be a jack of all trades if you have older computers. They may need minor adjustments from time to time such as replacing a mouse or switching keyboards. Learner will need assistance learning new skills, handling the mouse with ease, saving and printing their assignments.

It is advised to take attendance each week. Attendance is not mandatory but for those that attend regularly, you may reward them in some small way.

Learners that come to class on a regular basis tend to progress noticeably in their skills. Those that come on an irregular basis will forget many of their skills. It is very rewarding to see the progress each learner is making due to your dedication.

Special Needs for Computers

Most computers have very small fonts when you turn them on. It is advised to go to default and change the font size to 18. Some visually impaired learners may even function best at font size 26. Their assignments will need to be enlarged also.

Under Control Panel on most computers there is an option called Accessibility Options. Here you can adjust windows for your visually, hearing and mobility impaired needs. This allows you to change the screen resolution, use Microsoft magnifier. It will slow down the speed of the mouse. You can increase the time when the computer goes idle when the keyboard is not in use The are other aides available on the market for visually impaired learners such as a keyboard with larger print letters. Such a keyboard makes it so much easier for the learner to find the letters. Also there are letters that can be applied to the keyboard.

On your computer under the function, Control Panel, you will find Accessibility Options. Here you can make adjustments

for your learners for the monitor, text and color of your screen, hearing impairment or change your mouse options.

Programs Available for Learners

There are many programs available for those people who are learning to use the computer. Due to copyright laws, we are not recommending any specific program, just generally suggesting types of programs that are available.

Some programs provide very basic help with spelling short words. There may be points or music as a reward system for spelling a word correctly. Numerous programs are available for distinguishing small and capital letters of the alphabet.

One word of caution, many basic programs are geared to children and some adults will take offense to working on a program designed for a child.

Learners respond to realistic pictures from flyers from grocery stores or other department stores. We have pretend money that we work with to help them understand what it would cost to buy these items. Many of them are progressing nicely in understanding concepts of what costs $5 or less, $20 or less and items that are very expensive. They do enjoy using the money to buy large items such at TVs and Stereos.

We have discussed what comprised a healthy meal and a healthy diet for the day. Many of the math programs range from basic adding two single column numbers to adding triple column numbers. For a person who is extremely adept in math but is limited in his or her writing capacity, there are programs which are very challenging and fast paced. Any program that involves the understand of adding money is always a hit with learners. If the program is too easy, they take pride in knowing the answers. Any life skill gives these individuals a feeling of being worldlier and less isolated.

Everyone likes and deserves a challenge in life. Everyone can learn something new according to their level of learning with encouragement and praise. It is important to keep a volunteer program of this nature going in a consistent manner. Those involved appreciate the help, those who volunteer feel the rewards.

Student's Original Works

These are examples of student's works that they typed.

Sometimes it was necessary to write down their thoughts and they typed from a handwritten paper. These learners are intellectually challenged. They have hopes and dreams like anybody else might have. We want to give you some ideas of things to do with a word processing program and very basic learners. Sometimes they may tell you their thoughts and you may need to write them out by hand before they are typed out. A few are able to type on their own. For a very basic Computer learner, they may only know how to find the letters that spell their name. It gives them great pride to have a piece of paper that came from the printer that has their name on it along with a picture. It makes them feel they are part of the computer age. I had one student who wanted me to type letters to her cousin. She was able to write but she wanted her letters to sound professional. She was thrilled to see her thoughts typed on paper. Her cousin would send her self addressed and stamped envelopes.

These are just a few of the examples of ideas from very basic students that I have worked with over the years.

Last night I went to College . Mike learned Life Skills and

Mike wants to be a Doctor and wants to work hard at

School so Mike could make better life for himself so he could make $60,000 a year &wants to be independent, & live on my own someday & have my own apppartment.

Those are my goals to work hard for so I can meet my goals

& achive them in 10 years time. Mike would like to be rich

have a girlfriend whom one day I will marry.

When I'm thinking at night

Can't even think of the words

just the music

soon the song

but I am still missing something ………….. the verse

I got my hair and my face done. They used blow

dryer and curlers. They put cream on my face. They

used shampoo and rise. I going to the school. saw

Teacher at school. Short drive. In the van. Back to

Venture in the van. Have a good day

the fireworks were cancelled

but they will be back tomorrow night

my favorite authors are stephan king and john grishom

I WANT TO PLAY THE GUITAR. I WOULD LIKE TO

TRAVEL. I WANT TO LEARN MORE ABOUT

COMPUTERS.

I went to Bingo with Judy and Brenda

We all won some money. I will buy a scratch ticket.

I want to win the Jackpot. I will buy the Large T.V. with that

money.

I went shopping with Jennifer we bought groceries. I helped pick out celery. The celery was nice and green and firm . We put the celery in a salad . We bought eggs fo making scrambled eggs. We bought milk and

oranges. After we found everything we went to the check out counter . I helped load the groceries in the van.

Here a learner typed what was on the screen.

With this skill, they learn to find letters on the keyboard.

WE ARE MOVING INTO

WE ARE MOVING INTO

A NEW HOUSE.

A NEW HOUSE .

Writing memos, being involved in important daily functions makes a learner feel important

To : All workers and staff

Our workplace will be closed on Labour Day, Monday, Sept I.

We will reopen for business Tuesday, Sept 2.

Thank You!

If you have access to the internet, learners love to send emails to email pals, friends or relatives. Once and individual has learned the keyboard, it is easy for them to type out a message that has been pre- written on a sheet of paper. They love checking to see if they received and answer to their messages.

Suggested Topics for Small Classes

What is important to your group of learners? Here is an outline of possible topics to choose from.

1. Getting Started
   a) Review of letters, sounds of letters , sight words and basic number skills
   b) This is to see exactly what level the learner is functioning at

2. What Time Is It

a) Time, clock, time concepts related to everyday life

b) Using a watch, reading time tables, bus schedules

3. Dates

a) Dates, calendars holidays

b) Using g a calendar, writing down important dates

c) Keeping track of Dr's appointments, birthdays, outings

4. Money Skills

a) Coins, bills, paying bills

b) Cost to buy items, getting change

5. Greetings

a) Social greetings, expressions, feelings, signs

b) How to behave in various situations

6. Prices

a) Reading prices, receipts, sales items, getting a good deal on items

7. What We Eat

a) Nutrition, choices, food safety, sanitation

b) Food preparation, recipes

8. Grocery Shopping

a) Names, selection, labels, prices, lists

9. Labels

a) Best before labels, reading labels, storage

10. Colors

a) Names, colors around us, coordinating

11. Telephone Numbers

a) Type names and phone numbers in columns

12. On The Move

a) Reading maps, bus, directions, distance

13. Eating Out

a) Fast food, nutrition, menu. Paying

14. How Much

a) Measurements, household, medication, weight, volume

15. Keeping Well

a) Body exercise, health, regular checkups, when something feels wrong

16. At Home

a) Appliances, tools, safety. Electrical cords

17. On the Job

a) Terms used at work, safety, coming to work on time

18. Don't do it this Way

a) Following instructions

19. The computer

a) Having fun at the computer, word processing, learning programs

Preparing Assignments for a Classroom Setting

Each learner will progress at his or her own pace, complete assignments and want to socialize during class. For a one to two hour class, a one page assignment allows for time to socialize and complete the assignment. Make assignments achievable and know your learners.

One learner may find a full page too overwhelming, ½ page may be more appropriate for them. For a learner who has trouble finding his spot on the page, the paragraphs should be very short and spaced apart. For someone who has a visual problem, the font size may need to be increased, even as high as font 28.

A learner who does not know his small case letters would be able to complete the assignment if it was written in all capital letters. In time it may be possible to introduce a few small letters amongst the capital letters In MS Word it is very easy to change the case of the assignment Format and change case to Upper Case.

Many are able to type their assignments well although they are unable to read what they have typed. Make sure you print each person's assignment for them to take home.

Some like to keep their assignments in a notebook and others will just fold it and put it in their pockets. The printed assignment, no matter how much they typed, gives the learners great pride of accomplishment in class.

Clear Writing

Reading material we take for granted in our everyday living
is written at a level that many can't read. A few of these
reading materials include the newspaper, cooking directions
and reading directions to take medicine.

Adults that do not have good reading skills are still interested
in understanding these . It may be necessary to rewrite an
article of interest or cooking recipe in a simpler form. Here
are some hints that may help in this process:

- Substitute three and four syllable words with one and two syllable words
- Keep each sentence as short as possible
- Keep Paragraphs short with spaces in between each one.
- Use a larger Font, preferable size 18 or bigger
- Do not provide too much new information on a page

Here is an example of an article found on the internet
and the rewrite that can be used in an assignment.
Notice that the second article contains the same
information but is written in a simpler form to read.

Before You Walk Alone in the Dark

From Tina Kells

There is evil in the world. As children we are taught to fear the "boogeyman" and be wary of human strangers. We are given images of danger that are intangible and unrealistic. The sad fact is that the creatures we have to fear the most are not imaginary beasts but real life people. How can one stay safe in a world of invisible threats? Having some basic street smarts is a good place to start!

There is safety in numbers.

It is always better to go out in a group of trusted friends than it is to walk alone. Whenever possible have at least one other person to walk with. If it is just not possible to have a "buddy" then stick to well-populated, busy areas. Avoid hidden trails, short cuts through secluded areas or lanes that are not well traveled. Stay in well-lit areas where there is traffic and other people on foot.

Walk with the light.

Stay in well-lit areas. Do not walk in dark parking lots, dark alleys, dark lanes, dark trails, or dark anything. A well-lit path in a well-populated area is your safest route to any destination, even if it takes a bit longer. Afterall, is your personal safety worth risking for a few saved minutes? Wearing reflective clothing is a good defense against invisibility, but you need to be sure that the reflective areas are large enough and are exposed from every angle. Do oncoming cars see you, but not those at side streets?

Do You Walk Alone at Night?

There is evil in the world. Children are taught to fear strangers. There is danger we can not touch. It is sad, we

fear other people the most. How can we stay safe? Here are some rules to keep us safe at night.

There is safety in numbers.

It is better to walk with friends. It is not safe to walk alone. Have one person to walk with Do not walk alone at night. If you do not have a friend to walk with, stay in busy areas. Do not take short cuts. Do not walk where there are no lights. Walk where there is other traffic.

Walk with the light

Stay in an area where there are lots of lights. Do not walk in parking lots. It does not matter if it takes a bit longer to get home. Your safety is worth that extra minute. Do not wear dark coloured clothing. Wear something that reflects light. Cars need to see you,

Goal Setting for Students

Students come to our computer lab with a wide variety of experiences. We need to assess what our students are capable of doing when they come to our program. At this time, we do not have a set method to evaluate a student that comes to our program on Monday afternoons. We have some very basic ideas as to what the student needs to learn in our class. We only have two volunteer instructors for a class that might be as large as 10 students. They do not function at the same level.

We do our best. We come up with assignments that have various themes to them. We type out recipes, calendars, events, information about people that affect our lives. We try to make the topic interesting and relevant. There are learners that have difficulties completing the whole assignment. A shorter version is made for them. They may have difficulties concentrating or they get easily distracted. We will enclose a few examples of the two types of assignments.

Here is just one example of a student that types a big slower. In our program we can observe him for the first day and the following days. This student in our class enjoys typing.

He can sit by himself at the computer and follow the words on the page. We have designed activates for him to do for the next few weeks to bring him up to the level of the other students. We will need to review this chart each week.

Activity	Skills be practiced	Web site,
turning computer on with assistance	Turning the computer on and off independently	Superbowl site, watching the videos
Using the mouse	Navigating around a web site	Website watching different activities there
Finding a site on Google	Using a search engine	Finding a site of interest
Book marking a site as a favorite	Using a search engine	Browsing a site bookmarking it for future use

ASSIGNMENTS

Class Assignments

Here is a variety of assignments that have been used with learners over the past 13 years. They vary in degree of difficulty, subject such as grammar exercises, exercises in use of the computer, straight typing assignments and information your learners may have interest in. You know your learners best, what they might be able to handle now,

what they might be able to type after some practice. It can't be emphasized enough that they enjoy a challenge. Your

role is to help them along with their questions. You may want to start students with typing only ½ of an assignment. You may need to spend a few sessions getting them familiar with the various parts of the computer. We usually turn our computers on before class starts so they can start typing right away. You may want to go over start up procedures for a computer. They may catch on to a concept quickly or you may need to review it over and over. In many of these exercises we try to introduce new concepts.

These are examples of some exercises you may want to use. Feel free to adapt them or make up exercises of your own.

GRAMMAR

Punctuation

1. What mark goes at the end of most sentences?_____

2. What goes at the end of a question? _____

3. What goes before the s in a word to show that something belongs to something or someone?_____

4. What mark means a pause?_____

5. What marks go around something someone says?_____

6. What means surprise or excitement?_____

Type these sentences with the correct punctuation marks:

The game was won on Sunday

Did you enjoy the game

My team s best player was not there

Yes I found The game exciting

He said I found the game exciting

The game was exciting

Ways to Figure out Words

1) Look for words inside words.

Example: Monday has the word day inside of it.

2) Look for words that rhyme.

Example: mild, wild, might, flight

3) Look for compound words.

Big words that are made up of two smaller words.

Example: bedroom is made from the words bed and room.

4) Be familiar with word families.

Example: ate, mate, late, ate, date, fate, gate, rate, plate.

If the word looks familiar, try it starting with another letter.

5) In what context is the word used?

Read the whole sentence or paragraph. What makes sense?

6) Look it up in the dictionary

The instructions for how to say the word may help.

7) The root word can help with figuring out the word

Example: vowel-consonant-e makes the vowel long.

Two vowels together usually makes the long vowel sound of the first vowel. Beet, beat.

1) Use rules of phonics.

Example: vowel-consonant

9) Break words down with their prefix, root word, and ending

Example: apartment a part ment

10)   Divide into syllables and say one syllable at a time

Example: apartment a part ment

11)   Sound out groups of letters.

12)   Blend the sounds together.

You can also sound out each letter and blend sounds?

13)   Know the sight words, especially those used the most.

Making Changes

This exercise is to help you practice making changes and corrections quickly and easily.

Correct these sentences:

I went to store today.

Where were you when I called.

How do you spell "carefuly"?

Please do that me.

This adresz iswrong.

Cut, Copy and Paste

Put these in the correct order -

Monday

Friday

Tuesday

Thursday

Wednesday

Sunday

Saturday

Sort Alphabetically

Wilson   Jones   Brown   Black

McKenzie   Sorrell

Write the short form for each of these days of the week:

Monday_____ Friday_____

Tuesday_____ Saturday _____

Wednesday_____ Sunday _____

Thursday _____

Verb Selection

Read the following sentences and decide on the best verb form to complete the sentence.

1. I (walked , am walk , am to walk) to work this morning.

2. The path (is being , will to be , was) very smooth.

3. I (will be to close , will close) the door.

4. My son (is walking, was walked , has walk) with me

5. My friend (fall, are falling , fell) down twice .

6. Her daughter and friend (is going to stay , will to stay , are going to stay) until they finish work.

7. We already (will pick , did picked) up our books.

8. You and I (are do , will to do , will do) the same .

9. I'll catch the bus , when school (is to be ending, be end, ends) .

10. Her students (are catching, will be catch , catches) the bus tomorrow morning.

Add Endings to These Root Words

(Use tab key to make columns)

word -ed - ing -s

name   face

flame   base

taste

shape

age

Words that sound the same but have different meanings:

1. Is the boy a mail or a male? _____

2. Which hurts, a pain or a pane? _____

3. Does a clipper ship have sales or sails? _____

4. Which flies, a plain or a plane? _____

5. Is a story a tale or a tail? _____

6. Does a lion have a main or a mane _____

7. Is the light coloured pale or pail? _____

8. Which is icy, hail or hale? _____

How To Write Personal Stories

GETTING IDEAS,

- important dates/moments
- life changing events
- use photographs, keepsakes; letter; cards; mementos, journals or even your family and friends to get ideas

PRE - WRITING STAGE (Before you begin writing)

- be specific. Only write about a specific event
- close your eyes, repeat it over and again in head
- pretend you're telling the story to a friend
- if it helpful use a tape recorder to record your thoughts

PLAN –story could include.. Who? What? When? Why?

How?

- story must have a beginning . middle and end
- include your feelings about the event

WRITE and RE- WRITE

- write a draft
- show it someone to proof read

FINAL COPY

- type up the final copy

Canadians Overweight

People in Canada are not as healthy as they think.

Many Canadians fool themselves about their weight. When asked if they're overweight, 44 per cent said yes, with seven per cent admitting to being obese. The reality is worse.

Reasons for being overweight are lack of time, being tired most of the time and being stressed. People feel they lack the time and skills to prepare healthy meals. Researches shows insufficient sleep and stress actually change our metabolism and lead to cravings and changes in how the body stores energy.

Chief Tecumseh

In the war of 1812 Chief Tecumseh fought with the British helping the capture of Detroit. In the Battle of the Thames Tecumseh was killed and buried in a secret location.

Tecumseh was born in 1768 as a member of the Shawnee Indian tribe, native to Ohio. He had one brother, Tenskwatawa post, Keth-tip-pe-can-nunk, also known as Tippecanoe, thrived in lllinois' Wabash River Valley until 1791, when it was destroyed to make room for the white man.

In May 1808, Tecumseh and his brother left Ohio and founded the village Prophet's Town in the same location as the former Tippecanoe. The land had been claimed by the Potawatomi and Kickapoo tribes, but Tecumseh and his brother were granted settlement. Their village would eventually become the Indian equivalent to Washington, D.C., the capitol of a great Indian confederacy.

General Harrison and his men moved west to a site on a wooded hill farther away from Prophet's Town. Harrison warned his men of a possible invasion from the Prophet, although Tecumseh had told his brother not to attack the battle-ready white men until the Native union was strong and completely balanced.

COMPUTER SKILLS

Computer Class - Progress:

Student can demonstrate that he or she can:

1. Start computer on own

2. Access programs

3. Use programs

4. Quit programs

5. Shutdown computer

6. Reach personal goals typing

7. Use mouse

8. Use Windows

9. Word processing- change cursor position, arrow keys,

backspace, delete, highlight, bold, italics, underline, copy,

cut and paste, print, fonts, spell check, save

Can do on own:

Start

Shutdown

Enter & Arrow keys

Space bar & Enter

Point & Click Mouse

Typing - name, capitals, type from another source, Delete &

Backspace

change font size (size 18 is easier for him to see)

typing is slow but accurate

Learning programs - math, spelling, phonics, likes to try out

new learning programs

Can do with minimal assistance:

Save As to disk, Print document

Access programs

CD ROM

Has difficulty with double-click

Can concentrate two or more hours while working on

computer, usually works on 3 or 4 different activities during this time

Tab Keys

Use the tab key to make columns:

snap wall mail back hail

home high low sink set

was major class want tool

Fill in the missing vowel to make a word:

m__n	h__lp	m__p	h__t	co__t
f__t	dr__p	l__ke	n__se	e__t
c__n	tr__p	n__t	me__t	s__t

Ran	Can	Run	Come
Sign	when	Yams	Gun

I do not have a _____.

I like to eat _____.

I_____ to the store.

_____ you swim in the pool?

I saw the house had for a sale _____.

My sister _____ to school when she is late.

_____ can we get together for coffee?

Save. Click on Print Preview. Are all the columns straight? Does this all fit on one page? Make changes before printing

Internet

Turn on the computer by pressing on the power button. Wait for the desktop to come up.

Steps to use the internet:

- Double click on the internet icon. You can also right click the mouse once and then left click once on Open.
- It will open on Google.
- If you know the exact address, put the mouse in the address box, click once and type it in. Press Enter. Your site will come up.
- If you are searching for information put the mouse in the search box, click once and type it in. Press Enter.
- Choose a site by placing the mouse on one.
- When the mouse shape changes to a hand with a pointing finger click once. Your site will come up.
- Navigate through the website by clicking on topics.
- To go back, click on the large back facing arrow in the top left corner of the screen.
- When you are done click on Home, which is a picture of a house.
- Click on file, Exit to get off the Internet.

 To shutdown the computer, click on Shutdown at the bottom at the screen. Turn off the monitor.

The internet can be used to find information.

Sites that you want to visit over and over again can be put on the Favorites list. By putting it on the Favorites list it will be easier to get to.

Watch for the green check mark to see if a site is safe to go on.

You can use the internet to do email.

Saving Money

1. Do an article on Word about saving money.

2. Give a way to save money in each of these categories:

Food, Clothing, Shelter and Transportation.

3. With each suggestion give an example.

4. Content should be easily understood and expressed with

correct grammar and punctuation,

5. Tables, graphics, etc. may be used.

6. Restrictions:

a) No less than half a page and no more than one page

b) Font - use size16, use a suitable font , but not Times New Roman

c) All margins - .75

d) Title - make up a suitable title, Centered & Bold

e) Body - Fully Justified

f) Spell Check

g) Save

7. Check your work on-screen before printing.

8. Proofread after printing; make corrections & changes.

Do your best job you can before saying it is complete.

Skills Checklist

Using the mouse & computer basics: parts of the computer

Start up

Using the mouse, accessing programs

Point and click

Double click

Click & enter

Drag, Scroll

Minimize and maximize windows, box with X

Title bar, menu bars,

Toolbars, buttons. Status bars

Drop down menus

Dialog boxes

On- screen messages

Shutdown

Word processing

Caps

Wordwrap

Format, font size, bold, underline, italic

Delete, backspace

Spell check

Justification, margins

Save to disk, file name

Open and close documents

Print preview, print

Keyboard commands enter, command, line

Default

Arrow keys, home, page up & down

Cursor, I-beam

Ctrl + home

Font size and type

Highlight/select

Orientation,

Insert/sort/bullets/table insert graphics

Cut, copy and paste

Help

Icon/shortcut screensaver

Desktop

Hardware/software

Mouse-left, right,

Center

Manuals

Using the Internet- Basic Skills

Use mouse

Log-on to internet

Recognize web address

Type in address

Location and click on links/ scroll

Enlarge print

Use command buttons

Use bookmarks & use of history

Use favorites & add to favorites & organize

Use search engines & directories

Print a web page or portion of a page

E-mail

Log-in

Start personal e-mail account & password

Write and send a message

Receive and read new e-mails

Reply to emails received

Exit e-mails

Save and delete message

Save addresses

Attachments

Greeting cards

Troubleshooting and installing a Program

The Internet

Most of you have used the internet to send e-mail and some of you have looked at sports websites. In the next few weeks we want you to learn how to get on the internet to look up things.

We have only one computer connected to the internet so you will be taking turns going on it. Let us know what topics you are interested in looking up. Do you want to look up a favourite singer or movie star? Would you like to find out more about your favourite hockey team? Are you interested in gardening or cooking? Do you like to look at pictures of dolphins? Whatever your interests are, we can guide you to websites to find more information.

To connect to the internet double-click on the Internet Explorer icon - a big blue e.

Wait for the internet home page to come up.

When the home page is up, type the address of the website in the Address Bar.

Press Enter. When the website is loaded, you can scroll down the page using the scroll bar. You can go to other pages by clicking on other key words usually listed on the left of the screen as well as near the

top of the screen. You can click wherever the mouse pointer

becomes the shape of a hand.

If we do not have an address for a specific site, you can

search for information by entering your topic of interest in the web browser. This is the blank space in the middle of the screen.

As you are going through a site you can go back to a

previous page by clicking on the arrow at the top that is

pointing left. If there is something you wish to print let us know.

When you are finished, click on the Home button at the top of the screen. It looks like a house.

How to close the internet

Click on File.

Then click on Exit.

Or click on the x box at the top right of the screen.

You must always close the internet when you are finished unless

someone else is waiting to use it.

It is really quite easy to use the internet and once you learn how it can be a lot of fun. You can also look up a lot of good information that can be interesting as well as useful.

Email for those who use Yahoo

Our email address is_____ @ yahoo

To Get Messages:

1. Connect to Internet

2. In address box at top type in www.yahoo.com/

3. When the site comes up, click on the picture of the

letter near the top of the screen

4. When the sign in box comes in type in your user I.D.

5. Click in password box and type in your password

6. Click on sign in button or press enter on the keyboard

7. When the email comes up look for a message in the

center of the screen that tells if there are any new

messages. Click on this to get a listing of messages.

Or click on Inbox

8. To open messages, click on subject, where mouse

becomes a hand

9. To close a message, click on Mail Home or Inbox

10. To Send a message:

    Click on Compose Message

    Put the address in the TO: line

    Under the subject, Put the subject of the email

Write the message in the provided space

Click on Send button.

11. To Close your mail box

Click on sign out near top right of the screen

Then click on Sign Out Completely

Click on Home button on menu bar at top of screen

Blogging

I like to blog. It is a new means of expressing myself freely. The blog that I write on was created by a fellow author. He starts out writing about an experience he had as a young lad. Everyone can relate to his experience. He wrote about his first love. Blogs have rules. You need to follow a pattern. Anyone who happens to stumble upon this blog can read it.

This author is a professional writer. He has shown me a trick or two about writing. No matter what your trade is, it is always nice to have a friend who can help you. I am new at professional writing. I have a partner who proofs everything I write.

My new friend, puts a zing zag and a different angle or perspective on the way I see things. To quote him, now and again he forgets to put on his rose colored glasses. I have enjoyed writing for this blog. I can relate to the different topics he posts.

Who am I to be an expert in these fields? I never said I was, writing is just my thing. You will be amazed what you can write once you get your creative juices going. The thoughts just flow from your brain when you let your creativity flow free. As a blogger you know, your writing is not signed. You use a pen name. This means you need to log in, identify yourself. You sign in under the pen name you choose. You need to <u>copy a code number</u>. Nobody uses inappropriate language. is clean fun, a means to vent thoughts and you never know who might read it and leave a comment.

Some people come to read blogs and just leave a brief comment. Others read the blogs, think, wow, is this ever neat; they leave a bit more than a comment. Some people leave a long comment. The longest comment you can leave is 3000 word. It is easy to leave a 3000 comment in a blog.

When you are having so much fun being creative, your mind wanders and you even exceed the limit. Amazing, you have to rewrite your blog.

Devices we Use Today

Devices	Already Have	Would Like to Have	I need
Cell Phone What can you do on your cell phone?			
X Box			
DVD Player			
W II			
Super X Box			
Computer - What do you use your computer for?			
VCR			

Cell Phones

By Geraldine

Today many people carry a cell phone. This modern technology allows people to stay in touch with others no matter where they are. Many people who are thinking about getting a cell phone need to know there are many different cost factors.

You can have a phone that you pay monthly fees by companies called providers. These providers have different monthly packages for payment. Each company will try to make you think they are giving you a better deal. There are other fees such as activation fees. This is a fee to start up your cell phone. It is important to understand that some of these companies want you to commit to a contract up to three years.

Be very careful before signing any papers. They will keep you in a costly contract that you can't get out of. Some cell phones you can add money to each mouth and you are not tied to a contract.

If you need a cell phone, it is good to have one for emergency purposes. You could be in an isolated area and you might need to call for help. Some people spend too much time on their cell would tend to wonder what these people did before cell phones were invented. It is very dangerous to talk on a cell phone while driving a car. It distracts the driver from keeping a close eye on traffic. In the future, it might be a illegal to talk on the cell phone and drive at the same time.

Working with Photographs on Your Computer

Many people today use a digital camera. The pictures from them can go on your computer. The pictures can be sent by email to your friends and family. It is very important to keep track of the pictures you have downloaded onto your computer. If you want to see these pictures later, you need to know where they are. We are going to learn how to make new folders today. Each of your folders can be labeled. There is no set rule how folders should be labeled. They can be labeled by date or they can be labeled by the season of the year. Some people like to label their folders by the names. These can be the names of the people who have pictures in that folder.

Here is an example:

You may have lots of pictures of your pet or children. Start a new folder and label it, the name of your pet or child

Go to File on the upper left side of your toolbar.

Click on File, then click on new folder

The little box below the folder will turn a different colour

Start typing in the name you want on that folder

I would type in Shelley if I wanted a file of pictures of my daughter

When you have a folder, you need to remember where the folder is. It is common for people to put folders in the section of the computer called My Pictures If you have your pictures in the folder, then my pictures, it is easy to find them.

For lost pictures on your computer, you just need to go to My Pictures. You will see single pictures in that file. Click on the picture and drag it to a folder. You will not have any trouble finding pictures.

If you want to email a picture, go to your email site. Write in the name of the person who is getting the email. You will see on the page a little paper clip. Click on that symbol to get your picture. When you click on the paper click you will see My pictures

At this point you can browse in the new folder you made to find your picture.

LIFE SKILLS

Fire Safety In The Kitchen

Stay in the kitchen when you are cooking.

do not lie down or sleep

do not leave home

don't let handles of pots stick over edge of stove.

be extra careful if heating any type of oil

Turn off burners and oven on stove when you are done

unplug appliances.

Wipe appliance after a spill.

Clean stove top and ovens regularly.

Grease can catch fire easily.

Loose sleeves or clothing can catch fire leaning over a stove or if it dangles close to burners.

Store pot holders and towels away from stove.

Curtains must not be near stove.

Use pot holders to lift pans and remove food from the oven.

If a pan of food catches fire,

carefully slide a lid over pan

turn off stove burner.

Keep lid on until pan is cold.

If the flames do not go out right away,

call the fire department.

If a fire starts in the oven,

close the door and turn off the oven.

Don't plug in too many appliances

to the same electrical outlet.

Keep appliances away from walls or curtains.

Replace frayed or cracked cords.

Don't use damaged plug or out

Don't get appliances wet inside

To take food out of a microwave always uses pot holders.

Remove lids or plastic from food very carefully,

away from yourself to prevent steam burns.

Make sure food is not too hot before eating.

If anything catches fire in a microwave,

keep the door closed and turn off or unplug it.

Have it checked before using again.

Run cool water over a bum for 10 to 15 minutes.

Do not use butter.

If skin is blistered see a doctor right away.

If clothing catches on fire, stop, drop to the floor, cover your face with your hands, roll over and over to smother flames. Do not run.

Safe Medication Use

Know what you are taking and why- ask about side effects.

Keep medications in original containers so that you and

others know what they are.

Go to the same pharmacy for all of your medications so that your pharmacist knows what you taking. Find out where to store your medications: some need to be kept in a cool dry place, while others are kept in the fridge.

Ask if it is safe to drink alcohol while on medications. Give expired or outdated medications to your pharmacist to dispose safely. Keep medications out of reach of children and pets. Talk to your pharmacist about over the counter medications to see if they are safe for you.

Talk to your pharmacist about difficulties with:

- Opening medication bottles;
- ask about containers that open easily.
- The print on your prescription bottles-
- if it is too small ask for larger print.

Forgetting to take your medications.

- Ask your pharmacist for a weekly medication dosette that organizes your pills by day and times.

Reading a Newspaper

A daily newspaper in a city has many pages and section.

Look at the first page of the paper. It has the main news

stories of the day . The headline is in large print. The

bigger the news story. The headlines can help you find

the stories you want to read .

Each news story tells five things. They are the five W's

They are who, what , where , when and why. News

stories give facts about what has happened in your city

the country and the world.

The family life section has stories about food, clothes,

Health and other things of general interest. In the entertainment section

you can find stories and listings about TV and MOVIES.

The sports section gives information about sports.

Another section has ads about things for sale and jobs

in the community . This is the classified ad section.

The editorial pages have opinions where editors try

to get readers to agree with them. The letters to the

editor give people a voice in the newspaper.

Reading a newspaper helps a person keep up with what is happening.

Even if someone only looks at the pictures and reads the sports section

it can help a person learn new things and improve their reading skills.

Fuel up for Spring Sports

It's spring! The weather is getting nicer and people start spending more time outside. In organized spring and casual pursuits alike remember your body's spring training fuel needs.

Include plenty of carbohydrates to fuel your muscles. Smart choices include whole grains, fresh fruits, vegetables and beans

Eat carbohydrates throughout the day, before and after workouts and training sessions.

Include protein from lean sources like meat fish poultry, beans and dairy food and a moderate amount of fat.

Finally, remember to stay well-hydrated by drinking plenty of water and water -based beverages throughout the day.

As your activity level increases, increase your level of liquids.

Living With Diabetes

With a family history of diabetes and heart disease, 20-year old Cecelia really wanted to get healthy. Fad diets didn't work

Staying on track

I knew I'd reach my goal when I survived Christmas dinner with my family and still lost weight. It just takes planning. I prepared healthy dishes and still got everything I wanted even gingerbread men! I stopped thinking, "I can't eat this or that." I can eat anything as long as I make healthier choices the rest of the day.

I knew I had to change my life in order to really enjoy it. I kept envisioning the thinner, happier me and before I knew it, she was who I saw in the mirror. I've inspired my whole family and I have four friends who have all joined Weight Watchers after seeing my success.

No longer invisible

I'm no longer the invisible girl! I love my confidence and self esteem. Now I can walk into a crowded room and not have my eyes glued to the floor. Now that the weight is off I'm super confident.

 I couldn't be happier!

The Beginning of Summer

Summer is here! In many years, June 21 marks the official start of summer. The event is marked by an astronomical event– the summer solstice, the longest day of the year(with the most daylight), which occurs when the sun is farthest from the earth's equator. The season ends with the autumnal equinox (with day and night equal in length on September 22 or 23.

What does summertime mean to you? A long vacation from school? Swimming and ice cream cones melting in the sun? ON June 21 it's summer in the Northern Hemisphere, but in the southern half of the globe, it's beginning of winter! Summer is the season of greatest plant growth in areas with healthy summer showers. We have many farms that grow vegetables and fruit. For many farm workers, summer is a busy season filled with hard work under the hot sun.

Sunscreen

Prevent skin cancer by protecting the skin from burning by using sunscreen .

Use sunscreen that 30 SPF or higher.

put on 15 to 30 minutes before going outside.

Use lots of sunscreen.

Don't rub it in, let it soak in.

Put on all parts of the body that are not covered, such as

nose, ears, neck and feet. put on again after 2 hours.

Put on again after swimming or sweating.

Stay in the shade from 10 a.m. 4 p.m.

Wear a hat with a wide brim to cover ears and neck.

Wear clothes that protect you from the sun. Dark colours

are better than light colours. Don't wear cloth that you can see through.

Wear sunglasses that have UV protection.

When using insect repellant put on sunscreen first . After

20 - 30 minutes put on insect repellant.

Tips for Winter Safety

The outer layer should be waterproof.

Bundle up and dress in layers.

Remove inner layers if your body gets too warm.

Don't forget your mittens and a hat that covers your ears.

Wear Sunscreen.

Sun reflecting off snow and ice can cause sunburn.

Replace wet clothes with dry ones.

Watch out for frostbite.

Beware of the wind-chill factor and dress for the colder weather.

Identity Theft - Protect Yourself

Keep a record of your financial and credit card accounts, including numbers and expiration dates, in a secure place.

Review and then shred or destroy credit card statements once you no longer need them for tax purposes.

Only carry necessary credit cards or ID documents with you.

Cut up all expired and unused credit cards; the numbers may still be valid.

Never give credit card numbers over the phone to someone you don't know.

Make sure that any business with which you share your confidential information destroys it before discarding it.

Encourage your employer to destroy personal information before it is discarded.

Don't let personal information fall into the wrong hands.

Shred or destroy monthly Statements.

Phony Charities

Charity Scams 101 :

What is difference between a legitimate and a phony charity?

Keep informed about a charity and the work it does ,

carefully look at the charity, s full name .

Some scam artists use copycat names similar to legitimate charities .

If the caller asks me for personal or financial

information over the phone , should I hang up ?

Yes, Only give personal or financial information over

the telephone if you have placed the call and know the organization you are calling .

Should I ask for a tax receipt for my donation?

Yes, If the caller refuses to offer a receipt , make sure you understand

why before you consider making a donation .

What else should I look out for?

 High - pressure tactics, vague answers to your questions

P. O . Box addresses are all signs of scams

If someone comes to your door and claims to represent a charity,

Call the local chapter to confirm the fundraiser's identity.

Shopping at the Grocery Store

When you go to the grocery store, do you ever look up at the

signs to see where to find what is on your list? Each aisle in

the grocery store has a label. This label says what you can

find in that aisle. This exercise is about finding grocery store

items . You will need to insert a table to complete this exercise.

Go with your mouse to the top where it says Table, Insert, table. You will

be asked how many rows and columns you want in the table.

Click beside number and backspace or delete the old

numbers and put in 5 for columns and 6 for rows

In the top row type

Dairy	Pasta	Cereal	Bread Products	Fruit and Veg

Here is a list of food items.

Please put them under the right heading in the table.

Noodles   beans   hot dog buns   Milk

oatmeal   Yogurt   vanilla

Kraft dinner   Special K   oranges   Spaghetti

Eggs   Bagels   lettuce   sour cream   apples

Corn Flakes   muffins   tomatoes   rolls

Power Outage

Things to have handy at all times in case of a

power outage

1) Flashlight

2)Spare batteries.

3)Gas in the car

4) Bottled water

5) A battery operated radio to hear the news and warnings

6) Water in pots if water needs to be boiled

7) Crackers

8) Peanut Butter

9) Bread

If the power goes out throw:

1) Lunch meat

2) Any refrigerated foods that have warmed up

3) Foods that contain mayonnaise

4) Dairy products

5) Freezer items that have thawed

Things to do:

1) Unplug appliances for when the power come back on

2) Turn off the air conditioner

Food Safety Basics

Wash hands before, during and after handling food. Wash hands for 20 seconds and use soap.

Keep foods at the proper temperature when storing food.

Avoid cross-contamination by keeping raw foods away from cooked and by using separate utensils for raw and cooked food.

Use a meat thermometer to determine correct temperature for meat.

Once opened or cooked, store in air-tight containers especially designated for food.

Cool and refrigerate immediately. Date leftovers. If in doubt, throw out.

Only microwave in approved microwave containers and use only microwave-safe plastic and plastic wrap.

Don't use that yoghurt container or Styrofoam takeout boxes.

When shopping go to the grocery store last and pick up your perishable and frozen foods last. In the cart don't let juices from meat, fish and poultry drip on any other foods. Bag these separately from other foods. Cleaners should be bagged separately from food.

In summary:

- Wash hands thoroughly
- Keep raw meats and ready to eat foods separate
- Cook to proper temperatures

Sanitation

Sanitation means keeping things clean. Sanitation means working in a clean manner. Sanitation is very important in a kitchen. If sanitation is poor, people might get sick from the food that is served.

Dishes, utensils, equipment and pots and pans must all be cleaned properly. Follow correct procedures. Use the right chemicals and follow the directions or instructions that you are given.

When should you wash your hands?

	YES	NO
1. After going to the bathroom	____	____
2. Before starting work?	____	____
3. Before handling clean dishes?	____	____
4. After blowing or touching your nose?	____	____

Joan works in a restaurant kitchen. She washes the dishes. The dishwasher is very large. Joan scrapes, sorts and stacks the dishes. Then she loads the dishwasher. At the clean end the final rinse is very hot. This is to sanitize the dishes. This will kill the germs. Joan always washes her hands before touching the clean dishes.

Joan reads the notes on the staff bulletin board each day. All new policies are posted. New procedures are also posted. This is how Joan knows when there are changes. Joan always comes to work on time. She gets along well with her fellow workers. -She cooperates with both her coworkers and her supervisors. Her supervisor rates how well she is doing her job. Joan has a good job. She is very happy at the restaurant where she works.

Where does Joan work?

Is Joan always on time for work?

How does Joan find out about something new at work?

Is Joan happy with her job?

Is Joan a good worker?

Why do you think Joan likes her job?

Flu

How to prevent getting the flu:

1. The best way to prevent getting the flu is to have a flu shot.

2. Prevent getting the flu by stopping the spread of flu

viruses. This is done by stopping the droplets when a

person sneezes, coughs and blows the nose.

People can stop the spread of flu in these ways:

.Cover a cough with a tissue or with the elbow

.Cover a sneeze with a tissue

.Avoid contact with contaminated objects that

people with the flu have touched such as telephones and door knobs

Wash your hands often

Wash hands good and use lots of soap and water

If you are sick with the flu, stay home

Add Regular physical Activity To Your Daily Routine

Along with a well-balanced eating plan, exercise is important for losing weight and maintaining your overall health. With planning, you can easily fit 30 to 60 minutes of aerobic activity into your routine most days of the week.

Aerobic activity includes walking, riding a bike, inline skating, ice-skating and dancing It is important to your health because it strengthens your heart, lungs and blood vessels. To increase your levels of aerobic activity, first decide which activities you enjoy and look at your daily schedule to see where you can fit these activities in.

If you are re- starting from little or no daily physical activity, plan for five to 10 minutes per day. Once you achieve that level, increase it every week by 10 minutes until you.re up to 30 to 60 minutes.

Shopping and Cooking Healthy Meals

Shopping for food :

When you shop for food , remember these tips to pick

foods that are good for you and taste good and that will

cost you less money :

Save Money :

Make a shopping list and plan meals for the week.

Check newspaper ads for foods on sale .

Eat before you go shopping . If you go to the store

hungry, you might buy things you don't need.

Keep a list of things you buy often so you can

compare regular and sale prices.

Use discount coupons only if they are for items that you really buy

Store - brand vegetables and fruits may be cheaper

than other brands . Watch for sales on bulk family packs

and refreeze them in amounts you will use .

Eat Healthy :

Read food labels very carefully to get information about

ingredients and nutrients.

Buy lean cuts of beef and pork . Look for the words "

round " or " loin" in the name for beef and loin or leg

for pork .

Chicken and turkey often cost less than other

meats , and they have less fat and fewer calories .

Buy fruit juices instead of fruit drinks , which are mostly water and sugar

fruit juice and tomato juice are better for your health

than soft drinks or alcoholic beverages.

Comparative Shopping and Use of Tables

This activity involves tables in either Word or Excel.

Bring in some colourful sales flyers or catalogs and have your learner do comparative shopping.

They can write the prices down in the table as shown below.

This is a good life skill exercise in comparative shopping as well as

 learning how the use of a table.

You can determine which items you want them to shop for or they

can decide themselves.

ITEM	SEARS	WALMART
SHIRTS	$ 20.00	$ 7.99
GLOVES	$ 20.00	13.00
SOCKS	$ 12.99	$ 8.00
SHOES	$ 139.99	$ 79.00
PANTS	$69.00	$ 15-40
T SHIRT	$7-10	$ 6.50
JACKET	$40.00	$27-100
SCARF	$ 10 .00	$ 3.00

ASSESSMENT

Assessment for New Learners

This was the assessment exercised used for new learners.

Stories, True or False

SCHOOL

Robert rides his bike to school. He rides fast. The times goes quickly. It takes him fifteen minutes. He carries his books in a bag on his back. He is happy that he does not have to ride the bus. He saves money.

Robert takes ten minutes to get to school T or F

He cannot take his books. T or F

He saves money by riding his bike T or F

LUNCH

Ann buys lunch at work. She pays two dollars for a sandwich and seventy cents for milk. She does not like apples, so she buys ice cream which costs fifty cents. She likes her lunch.

Ann makes her own lunch T or F

Ann likes apples. T or F

Ann's lunch costs $3.20 T or F

Assessment of Memory Recall

This is an exercise I designed in attempt to place students into a literacy program at the Windsor Public Library. It is important to know if a person has basic memory skill. This is a basic example of a short story and how a person may or may not remember the context.

Tell me about something funny or interesting that happen to you.

This shows if a learner has good recall about what he hears or reads.

True story, my daughter did have one of those white frogs and here is the sad tale of what happened to it.

I had a little white frog that swam in the water. We kept it in

a little fish bowl with a cover on it. The frog seemed to like

the fish bowl, it kept on growing. One day I forgot to put the

cover on the tank. I looked in the tank that night before I

went to bed and the frog was gone. I looked for that frog for

an hour. I never found the frog. I called the pet store the

next day. The pet store owner said you will never find that

frogs if it gets out. They just dry up somewhere and look like

a spider web.

1. Where did the frog live?

2. What happened to the frog?

3. Why did the frog get out?

4. Do you think I will ever find that frog, why?

Put these ideas in order of how they happened in the story

I called the pet store

The frog got out

The cover was left off the tank

The frog grew inside the tank

Numbers and Letters

NUMBERS AND LETTERS

Basic Letter sounds:

b	bird	buck
s	snake	smoke
r	rabbit	river
l	little	light
g	girl	grass
h	hot	hat
t	took to,	two, too
k	kids	kitchen
w	wind	window
z	zoo	zebra
d	doll	dollar
m	mother	marry
n	news	not
j	jay	jelly
p	pope	pop
q	queen	quarter
v	valley	violin
y	yell	yellow
c	cat come cents center	

Numbers Exercise

1. Write the numeral:

three hundred and sixty-five _____

seventy-two _____

seven hundred and thirty-two _____

one thousand and ten _____

2. Circle the number that is bigger:

65 72 103

1,070 780 870

6,666 6,566 6,667

3. Write the numbers for these amounts:

ten dollars and fifty-five cents _____

sixty-two dollars and seventeen cents   _____

fifty-eight cents _____ _____

sixty-two dollars _____

4. Circle the right answer:

One third 1/3 1/4 or ½

One quarter 1/3 1/4 or ½

One half ½ 1/3 or 3/4

Three quarter ½ 1/3 or ¾

You have 7 cans of orange juice in your freezer on Monday on Friday you only have 2 cans of orange juice left. How many cans of orange juice did you use?

Using Letters

Can you make words out of the following letters?

n	p	h
t	a	s
c	b	m

n	e	h	k
m	i	b	C
a	s	t	R

Holiday Gift Giving

That time of year is coming fast when we all must get our shopping done for Christmas. Plan ahead so that the holidays can be enjoyed. Make a list of who you want to give gifts to and then decide what to give each person. Decide how much can be spent on gifts and then don't go over your budget. Only spend what you can afford.
Watch for sales and bargains.

Some people shop all year long to get the best prices! Shop early. When you have to buy everything at the last minute you usually end up paying full price and spending more. The important reason for giving gifts is to let someone know that you are thinking of them. So, the amount you spend is not important. It is the thought that has gone into picking the gift that counts. A gift that you have made shows the person that you really care. Think about making something like cookies or a holiday ornament.

You can also give your time and work. Make a gift certificate on the computer. For example, if you don't usually do dishes you might give a gift of doing dishes once a week. You could offer to do other chores around the house. Or if you don't see a friend or older relative very often you might give the gift of visiting more often.
Be creative and have fun with your holiday gift giving!

New Years

Everyone likes to make New Year's resolutions. These are promises to themselves to do things that will improve their lives.

Here are some examples:

* to lose _____

* to eat more fruits and _____

* to quit _____

* to save more _____

* to get eight hours _____ a night

* to exercise every _____

* to visit _____ friends more often

* to feel _____ about myself

* to learn something _____

vegetables weight sleep

money smoking friends

new good day

One of my New Year's resolutions is to _____

****

Things I did over the Christmas Season:

* had a turkey dinner * ate too much

* put up a tree * watched a lot of TV

* went to a party * went to a concert or   game

* visited with friends * shopped for gifts

What did you do? Add details

Halloween in North America

Halloween has become a major folk holiday in the US and Canada.

"Trick or Treaters " go from door to door and collect candies, apples and other goodies.

Many of Americans and Canadians will decorate their homes and offices for Halloween.

Some interesting facts about the celebration of Halloween:

Halloween is the holiday when the most candy is sold.

It is second only to Christmas in total sales.

North Americans spend $21 million on Halloween candies yearly.

Halloween is the third-largest party occasion next to Christmas and New Year's Eve.

Halloween is the Number 1 season for selling funny greeting cards.

In North America, some 25 million cards are sold each year.

Opposites

big	little
fast	slow
hot	
large	
short	
black	
skinny	
happy	
rich	
young	
weak	
soft	
messy	

Fill in the Blanks

	Yes	No
I would like to see the fireworks tonight	____	____
I like to eat strawberries	____	____
I like to go swimming	____	____
I would like to travel to the country	____	____
I like to watch TV	____	____
I would like to travel in a spaceship	____	____

I want to _____ at this _____.

It is the one I like to _____.

Maybe I will find a story about a famous

_____.

Sometimes you can see a famous person in the

_____.

If I ever met someone famous I would be

_____.

A person I would really like to meet is

_____.

I would like to meet this person

because_____.

When I have nothing to do I like to

_____ .

My favorite meal is _____ .

I like to eat _____.

Look	person	play games
Woman	man	book
Cereal	go for a walk	read
Breakfast	movies	happy
Glad	lunch	sad
Chicken	watch tv	dance
Dinner	sandwich	corn

RECIPES AND OTHER ACTIVITIES

This is an activity where each member of the classroom adds a line to create a story. As you can see from this story, it can turn out quite well.

Mr. Bean is Funny

It.s really cold. Mr Bean is funny. He is very funny. He dances funny. He dances in the show.

He drives a bug. He drives to go shopping to buy food. He buys pita and broccoli.

Mr. Bean hates going out when it is cold. But he has to go to school. He goes to college in his bug. He takes acting classes. His dancing helps him act. He takes reading. He is good at reading.His car, the bug, is in good shape. He sometimes has car trouble and it goes putt putt, putt, putt. Then he kicks it. He should take it to a garage. He has money for repairs but he is too lazy to go to the garage.

Sometimes when he is late for the dentist he has to change in the car. He always puts his shoes on the roof of the car. The shoes fall off on the road when he takes off. Then he has to hop on one foot to get someplace.

This is why Mr. Bean is funny.

Beef Noodle Chop Suey

1 Pound ground beef

½ cup chopped onion

3 1/4 cup hot water

1 package Hamburger Helper noodlesdinner

1 can mixed Chinese vegetables, drained

IN 10 inch skillet, cook and stir meat and

onion until meat is brown: drain. Stir in

Water, noodles, sauce mix and

vegetables Heat to boil, stirring

constantly. Reduce heat, simmer

uncovered 10 - 15

Wrap It The Way You Like

Some time you get a your a chice as to what you want on your wrap sandwich, That is what we are doing today. You get to decide what you want to roll into your flat bread Here are the your choices.

1 chicken

2 Lettuce

3 Pineapple

4 Tomato

5 Bean Sprout

6 Ranch Dressing

7 Sour Cream

What did put in your Wrap?

Breakfast in a Minute

Busy morning schedules are often to blame for skipping breakfast Try one of these quick breakfast options that are packed with nutrients:

Ready – to- eat cereal topped with sliced bananas and yogurt. Bran muffin and yogurt topped with berries.

Peanut butter on whole – wheat toast and milk.

Pizza and a glass of orange juice.

Toasted whole – wheat topped with fruit and yogurt.

Lean ham on a toast English muffin with vegetable juice.

Breakfast wrap with cut- up fresh or canned fruit and low fat cream cheese

Picnic

Last Monday Our Computer Class Decided To Take a Break. We went on a picnic! We went to Jackson Park and found a shady spot with a picnic table. It was very nice under the trees. It wasn't too hot.

This is what we had for our picnic lunch:

lunch meat	carrots	pop
strawberries	tortilla wraps	celery
ice water	cookies	
shredded lettuce		lemonade

Supplies that we took included:

paper plates	napkins
tablecloth	plastic cups

I hope you have found this book useful.

Please let others know about it.

www.ingramcontent.com/pod-product-compliance
Lightning Source LLC
Chambersburg PA
CBHW080429060326
40689CB00019B/4442